WORLD OF ROT

Learn All about the Wriggly, Slimy, Super-Cool Decomposers We Couldn't Live Without

Britt Crow-Miller

Storey Publishing

Dear Reader,

Welcome to the world of rot. You've probably been here long enough to realize that our planet is home to some amazing, and sometimes amazingly weird, life-forms.

All this life is what makes the world wonderful, as in *full of wonder*. But it's also what makes it rotten. In fact, the life and the rot are closely connected. Rot can't happen without life, and life can't happen without rot. Okay, sure, but what does that actually mean? It means that the breakdown of living things after they die is what allows new life to flourish.

This book is about seeing our world for what it truly is: a wonderful world of rot. It's there all around us, and you (yes, you!) are part of it. But to notice what's hidden in plain sight, you have to slow down and open your eyes (and, sorry, sometimes your nose) to the important, disgusting, weird, often stinky, and always life-giving processes of decomposition.

Of course the rot doesn't happen on its own. It takes the work of a ton of animals, fungi, bacteria, and other organisms. These decomposers are your neighbors, roommates, and sometimes even stowaways on and inside your body. It's time you are properly introduced.

Get ready to see things in a whole new way as you embark on a journey through the world of rot.

Curiously Yours,

Britt

Former Kid

Contents

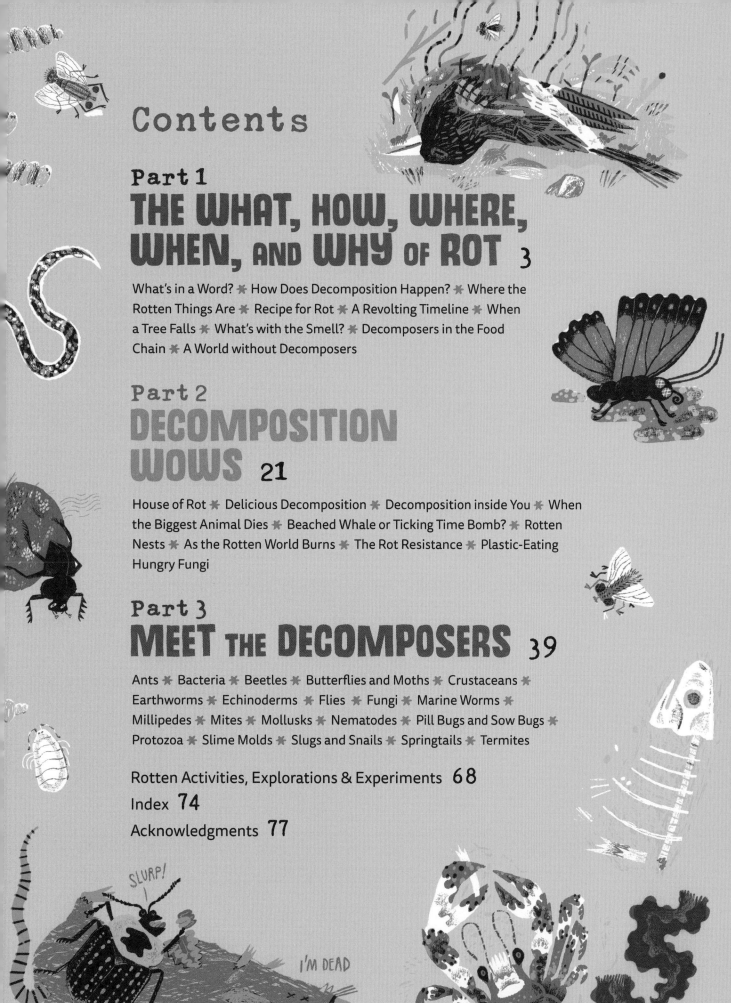

SLURP!

I'M DEAD

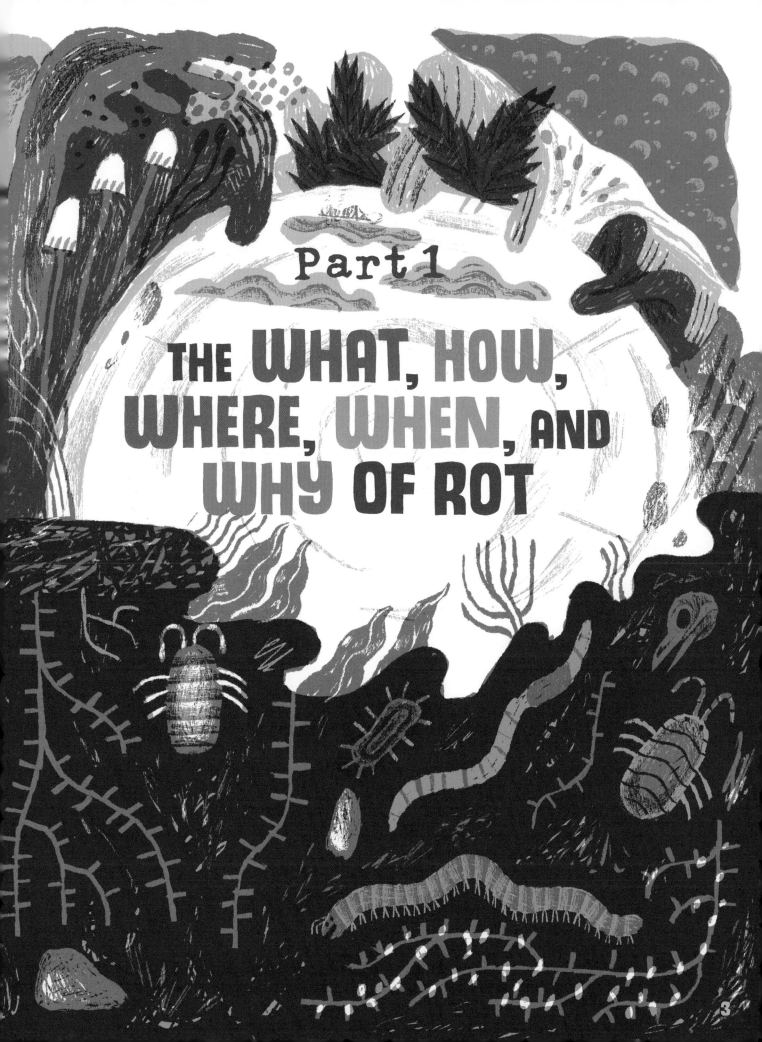

Part 1

THE WHAT, HOW, WHERE, WHEN, AND WHY OF ROT

WHAT'S IN A WORD?

COMPOSE (COM-POZE): to make something by putting things together

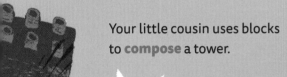

Your little cousin uses blocks to **compose** a tower.

Musical **composers** like Mozart and some of your favorite singers and bands arranged notes together to compose music.

Living organisms are **composed** of atoms like carbon, hydrogen, and oxygen.

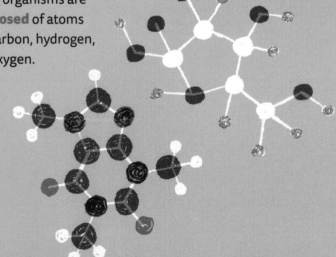

DECOMPOSE (DE-COM-POZE):
to break apart, rot, decay, disintegrate, putrefy

Just like when a tower of blocks falls down, when something **decomposes** in nature, it is broken down into different molecules. The building blocks of life are freed up to help make something new.

And just like composition, decomposition can't happen on its own. There are artists (yes, artists!) like mites and flies, fungi and bacteria behind the important process of recycling what's dead back into what's living.

HOW DOES DECOMPOSITION HAPPEN?

Decomposition is about breaking down organic matter. In this case, the word *organic* doesn't have to do with the special green label on some foods at the grocery store. Organic simply means something that was alive or came from something living. Animals are organic, and so is their fur, hair, skin, and poop. Plants and all their parts are also organic.

Imagine an apple growing on a tree. Like everything else in the universe, it's made up of molecules. A molecule of water, for example, is made up of two hydrogen molecules and one oxygen molecule. Apples are also made up of lots of other molecules, like sweet-tasting sugars made from combinations of carbon, hydrogen, and oxygen.

One day the apple falls to the ground.

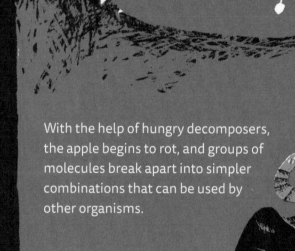

With the help of hungry decomposers, the apple begins to rot, and groups of molecules break apart into simpler combinations that can be used by other organisms.

H_2O GLUCOSE

But how does the breakdown actually happen?

The first way decomposers break things down is by eating the dead stuff. Organisms that do this are called **detritivores** (duh-TRI-teh-vors). These include snails, worms, and millipedes.

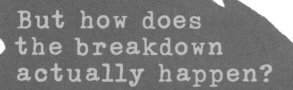

Dead stuff goes in.

Decomposed stuff comes out.

What about the decomposers that don't have mouths, like fungi and bacteria? These guys are known as **saprotrophs** (SAP-ro-trohfs). They ooze special proteins called enzymes onto their food. Mmm . . .

Enzymes break things down into simpler molecules that the saprotroph can absorb directly. No mouth, no problem!

Decomposers make important nutrients and building blocks like nitrogen, phosphorus, and calcium available for other living things to use, especially plants. They're the **living recycling centers** that keep this world going!

Are Vultures Decomposers?

Actually, no! They're scavengers. What comes out in their poop is still too big and complex to be recycled back into the soil.

WHERE THE ROTTEN THINGS ARE

Earth is teeming with life, from the thickest rainforests and the warmest seas to the driest deserts and the coldest tundras. Even the cities and towns most of us call home are bustling with beings other than human. With all this life, decomposers need to be on hand to help with the cleanup. Life is messy, after all.

Thankfully, members of the recycling crew can be found across nearly every square inch of the planet.

ROT

ROT

ROT

ROT

ROT

ROT

RECIPE FOR ROT

While things can rot any time, any place, and anywhere, there are certain ingredients that help to get things going.

1

Pour in 1 serving of dead or shed organic matter. Poop, hair, food, plants, animals, you name it!

2

Add 1 part oxygen. Most of the life-forms working on the front lines of rot need oxygen to live. Low oxygen levels just slow them down. This is why leftovers will last longer if they're sealed in a plastic bag or container.

O_2

H_2O

3

Spray in 1 part moisture. No living thing can survive without water, including decomposers. Think of mummies. These ancient Egyptian remains were intentionally dried out so they could be protected from decay. No water, no rot!

4

Add a sprinkle of hungry decomposers. Different kinds of decomposers prefer to munch and slurp and ooze onto different things, so make sure you pick the right guys for the job.

5

Bake at warm-to-hot, plug your nose, and wait for results. While some rotters like it warm and others like it hot, all decomposers will work in slo-mo (or not at all) if it gets too cold. Decomposition in the Arctic can take ages.

A REVOLTING TIMELINE

It might sound gross, but scientists and people who investigate crimes can use hints from decomposition, including when certain organisms show up at Café Decay, to figure out when an animal died. So next time you discover a songbird that made an unfortunate collision with one of your windows, put on a mask and consider doing some up-close detective work to look for clues about how long ago the animal went down for its permanent nap.

Five Stages of Animal Decomposition

STAGE 1

FRESH: Days 0—5

The moment an animal's heart stops beating, its body temperature begins to warm up or cool down until it matches its surroundings. After a few hours, its muscles become stiff. Though you can't see them, **bacteria** that made their home inside the creature when it was living are already diving into the dirty work of dissolving its organs. That's what friends are for, right?

Flies and other insect decomposers begin to arrive on the scene. Some of them, like **blow flies** (see page 53), lay their eggs in the mouth, nose, and ears of the carcass, so their babies will have something to eat when they enter the world. Thanks, Mom and Dad!

STAGE 2

BLOAT: Days 3—7

After several days, **bloat** sets in. This happens when the bacteria produce gases, inflating the body into a swollen balloon of skin, fur, feathers, or scales. The pressure builds until the gases find an escape route through the animal's nose, mouth, or poo chute. This is when things start to get seriously stinky.

Oh, and in case you aren't queasy yet, this is also when those fly eggs start to hatch into hungry, flesh-eating **maggots**.

STAGE 3
ACTIVE DECAY: Days 8–?

There's no way around it. Active decay is yucky. And . . . it's moving. This bird's feathery breast has burst open, all the liquids have drained out, and its insides are squirming and twitching with bugs and larvae. **The smell is at its peak.** This stage comes to an end when the little white fly maggots, now fat from feasting on flesh, migrate away from the body to make their cocoons.

STAGE 4
ADVANCED DECAY: Several weeks

At this point, the decomposers have done most of their work, recycling the calcium, nitrogen, hydrogen, and other nutrients from the animal's body back into the soil. **Larger insects** equipped to chew on the harder bits—like dry skin and cartilage—crawl in to finish the job. Other organisms begin breaking down remaining fur, feathers, and hair.

STAGE 5
SKELETONIZATION

Only bones and dry skin remain. There may be new plant growth in the area thanks to the nutrients the recycling crew successfully returned to the soil. Beetles, moth larvae, and mites may still be poking around to clean up the last remaining bits. How long an animal takes to decompose, from start to finish, depends on how much oxygen, moisture, and heat there is, plus what decomposers are present.

WHEN A TREE FALLS

It's not just dead animals that decompose. But rotting plants are way less disgusting and usually don't smell foul enough to make your eyes water.

Still, a single deciduous tree may grow hundreds of thousands of leaves each year, and every fall, those leaves, well, fall. Without decomposition, they would just pile up on the ground, year after year. What's more, the soil actually needs the nutrients locked up in those leaves in order to feed plants and other organisms.

Fortunately, thanks to fungi, bacteria, and various creepy-crawlies, most leaves will be totally recycled back into the soil within a year of falling. **But what happens when a whole tree dies?**

Fungi send out networks of rootlike tentacles called `hyphae` (`HI-fee`) over the wood (see page 54). Like tiny doses of barf with magic dissolving powers, enzymes leak from the tips of the hyphae and begin to break down the tree into carbon dioxide, water, minerals, and nutrients for the soil.

Mushrooms are the fruiting bodies of certain fungi. They produce spores so that the fungi can spread.

13

WHAT'S WITH THE SMELL?

Our noses can offer big clues when it comes to decomposition. The sweet, earthy smell of leaves decaying lets us know when fall has arrived. A waft of fruity mildew can remind us that, no, we never did find that banana in the back seat of the minivan.

While some smells are just mildly icky, other smells blow straight into putrid territory, causing people to wretch, gag, and run screaming after a single sniff. The whats and whys behind some of those foul smells might surprise you.

Low Tide

You might already know the smell of low tide at the beach. If you close your eyes, you might imagine a heap of rotten eggs festering inside a sewer pipe. **But where does that smell come from?** Oceans, especially their shallow parts, are teeming with life, which means they're also full of dead stuff. As these things decay, they release a stinky gas. When the tide goes out and the decaying matter is exposed to air, those gases escape.

Dinner-Bell Smell

Ever driven by some roadkill on a hot summer day? Rotting animals stink. These smells mostly come from the gases produced when bacteria and other decomposers break down the fats and tissues of the dead. **Different stinky gases are present in each phase of decay**. When a new odor kicks in, the aromatic dinner bell will ring for a new group of decomposers, on and on until the feast is over. If this process were odorless, decomposers wouldn't know where to go!

Smells to the Rescue?

Certain smells of animal decay can serve as a powerful signal to other animals to **stay away**, keeping them out of what might be a dangerous situation—after all, a fellow critter has somehow ended up dead. Smells can also come to the rescue when it comes to spoiled food. If the spoonful of slop you're about to put into your mouth smells gross, you'll probably think twice about eating it, right?

Rotten Copycats

Not all rotten smells come from rotting things. Plants like the **corpse lily** and the blossoms of the starfish cactus mimic the smell of rotting flesh to attract flies that will spread their pollen. Gifting these plants to your mom on Mother's Day is not recommended.

Little Oxygen, Big Smell

With some big exceptions (ahem, potatoes and cabbage), decaying plant matter doesn't usually have an intense smell. Feel free to stick your nose up close to a rotting apple or pumpkin. It's really not that bad.

But if decaying plants get too wet in, say, a backyard compost pile or a bog, things can take a stinky turn. That's because water can keep oxygen out, and the special bacteria involved in airless decomposition (called **anaerobic bacteria**) are known to make some super-stinky gases.

DECOMPOSERS IN THE FOOD CHAIN

Food gives living things the energy they need to survive.

The energy held in each link of the food chain moves up and up and up, from the patch of grass that feeds the rabbit to the fox that eats the rabbit to the bear that eats the fox.

UH OH

Green plants transform sunlight, water, and carbon dioxide into a tasty meal. Because they make their own food, these plants are called **producers**. They are the first link in every food chain.

The critters that eat up parts of those green plants form the next link of the food chain as **consumers**. In a forest food chain, these would be animals like fluffy bunnies, little brown mice, cheery songbirds, and most insects.

Finally, at the top
of the chain are the
apex predators, the
big cheeses with
big teeth, who eat
whatever suits them.

Of course, the snakes,
foxes, and bug-loving
woodpeckers that make up
the next link of consumers
in the chain need to eat,
too. They dine on plant-
eating consumers.

YOU'RE ALL FOOD TO US!

But wait.

There's one more super-important piece of the puzzle: **decomposers.**
When that bear at the top of the food chain dies, its body is a big, bulky
mass of locked up-energy, including the energy from the foxes it ate,
the rabbits *they* ate, and the grasses *they* ate. The same is true when
something from any part of the food chain dies.

**The decomposers take care of it all, unlocking the nutrients the
ecosystem needs to build new life. And so it goes, on and on, over
and over.**

A WORLD WITHOUT DECOMPOSERS

Think of all the stuff that rots. Crunchy fall leaves, cut flowers, leftover food. Now imagine a world piled high—unbelievably high!—with these things. Add layer after layer of massive tree trunks, plus mountains of dead-skin flakes, fingernail clippings, and shed hair . . .

Can you imagine walking over huge dead dinosaur carcasses on your way to school?
Without rot, the dinosaurs would still be here (along with the corpses of every creature and person that ever lived). Not a pretty picture.

Let's not forget the poop! A single person can produce more than 25,000 pounds of poop throughout their lifetime. Without decomposition, all the turds that have exited your body and the bodies of every other person and animal ever to live would just be lying around wherever they landed. George Washington's poop? Yup, right where he left it. Cleopatra's poop? Same.

Thankfully, though, things rot.

Where else are living things supposed to get stuff to build themselves out of? The grocery store?

Rot and the animals, fungi, bacteria, and other organisms that do the dirty work of decomposition are literally the **foundation of our world.**

Part 2

DECOMPOSITION WOWS

HOUSE OF ROT

You might think that decomposition happens only in gross places, but actually it happens everywhere, including in your own home. With a little bit of decomposition detective work, **you can get an up-close look at the rotten side of the world without even leaving the house.**

MOST WALLS are made of a powdery mineral called gypsum, sandwiched between layers of paper. If things are damp enough, a wall makes a very tasty meal for **black mold**. Black mold is not a fungus most would like to have among us.

DRY ROT caused by hungry fungi can make wood shrink, crumble, or even turn spongy. Too bad sponges aren't great for holding up houses.

TERMITES are wood decomposers. These hungry little log gluttons can enter homes through cracks and crevices.

IN YOUR BEDROOM, millions of microscopic eight-legged mites live in your mattress, on your blankets and pillow, and in your closet. They even live under your bed like actual flesh-eating monsters. *Flesh eating,* you ask? Yes.

Dust mites feed on dead skin cells from humans and other animals. A single person sheds up to 40,000 dead skin cells per minute. Without invisible armies of hungry mites, they would start piling up. And just to be extra gross, this also means we humans spend a lot of time rolling around in microscopic meadows of mite poop and dead mite bodies. Sweet dreams!

MOLDS AND MILDEWS can grow and spread on and in carpets when damp. See any little blue-green circles on the bottom of your rug? If so, there's a pretty good chance rot is at work.

ANTS sometimes follow the chemical traces of tasty decaying food morsels into homes. These insect decomposers also enter homes looking for water or a good place to nest.

Kitchen

Some of the big appliances we find in kitchens are all about avoiding decomposition. Putting food in the fridge slows down the rotting process, while sticking it in the freezer pauses it altogether. Next time your dad asks you to help put away the groceries, take a second to imagine what your kitchen might look (and smell!) like if you said no and came back a week later to check it out. Yuck.

FIND SOMETHING ROTTEN? Grab a magnifying glass and take a closer look. Why not put it in a bag and keep it around for a few days to see how it changes?

ONCE A MOLD SPORE LANDS on a piece of bread, it begins taking over, eating up the good stuff and helping along the rotting process.

DID YOU KNOW that the antibiotic you take when you get an ear infection, strep throat, or other bacterial infection is made from a mold called *Penicillium*? That's the same stuff that sometimes grows on old bread and cantaloupe. **Medicines made from mold have saved millions of lives!**

KNOW ANYONE WHO COLLECTS COMPOST? Most plant-based kitchen scraps can be composted. Take them out to a bin or pile, and decay will transform them into usable nutrients for the soil.

Bathroom

As the wettest room in most homes, bathrooms provide the perfect conditions for two familiar decomposers: yeast and mildew, both in the fungi family.

MILDEWS tend to be flat, rather than raised like other molds, and can look either fluffy or powdery. They can break down wood, paint, glue, fabric, paper, and even some materials used in the grout that holds tiles in place in walls and floors.

YEASTS like to feed on salts, sugars, and starches found in certain soaps, shampoos, makeup, and toothpastes.

SOME TOILETS flush into septic tanks, big underground basins used for storing waste when a house isn't connected to a public sewer system. Septic tanks are like **huge stinky guts**, working to break down waste with the help of decomposers like bacteria, fungi, protozoa, and nematodes.

DELICIOUS DECOMPOSITION

People all over the world eat fermented foods that wouldn't exist without the chemical changes that happen when things start to break down. If you've ever said yum to some yogurt, noshed on a slice of sourdough bread, or chomped on a crunchy pickle, then you, too, have eaten some delicious decomposing matter.

But let's be clear: fermented foods are not rotten foods. Not only are they perfectly safe to eat, but many are also considered super healthy. So what's the difference between a putrid cucumber on the ground in your garden and a dill pickle from the corner deli?

BARFY POISONING

NO!

DILL PICKLES

NO-SEY PICKLE

YES

When foods are left to rot on their own, the door is wide open to any decomposer that wants in on the job, including the ones that can have you running for the toilet.

Fermentation keeps the vomit vectors out by creating conditions where only particular decomposers are invited to join the fun, specifically certain oxygen-fearing bacteria, molds, and yeasts. Fermented food is considered preserved.

Hákarl

This Icelandic delicacy is made from fermented shark meat. Traditionally, the shark meat, which is toxic to humans before its transformation by bacteria, is buried under sand and rocks for several months and then hung to dry.

SHARKY?

Kimchi and Sauerkraut

For thousands of years, cultures around the world have been using certain bacteria to transform vegetables into tasty fermented side dishes. In Korea, kimchi (usually made with cabbage, spices, and other vegetables) is eaten at nearly every meal.

Stinky Tofu

This dish involves soaking tofu (soybean curd) in a strong-smelling mix of fermenting veggies, meat, milk, and herbs for days, weeks, or sometimes months. Fans often find it for sale by street vendors in parts of East Asia.

Yogurt

Yogurt is made when the right kind of bacteria get together with milk of any kind. Add some heat, let the bacteria get to work, and in just a few hours you'll have some yummy fermented milk, a.k.a. yogurt, to snack on.

Sourdough Bread

Sourdough bread doesn't use just any yeast to rise. It relies on a fermented mixture of flour, water, and wild yeasts found in the flour itself to get both its fluffy puff and tangy flavor.

Blue Cheese

What's the blue in blue cheese? Mold, of course! After a dose of mold spores is added to the recipe (yes, on purpose), the cheese is poked with sterile needles to create oxygen tunnels. Give it three or four months to ferment and, voilà, you'll have a delicious, mold-covered treat.

KOM BUCHA

DECOMPOSITION INSIDE YOU

Most people think of decomposition as something that happens out there, in forests, compost piles, and at the bottom of school backpacks. But . . . put your hands on your belly. Do you feel anything? Do you hear anything? Pay close attention, because—get this—**there is decomposition happening inside you at this very moment.**

Decomposers inside our own digestive systems break down the food we eat so the nutrients locked up inside those foods can get slurped up into our bloodstream, helping us grow and be healthy.

Bacteria Party!

Your large intestine may be home to up to 1,000 different types of bacteria. There are so many of them (trillions!) that all together they can weigh as much as 20 Kit Kat bars! They can also cause a lot of gas.

SURPRISE!

BUM-BURP MAKERS

20 PACK

Let's say you eat a big cheesy slice of pizza...

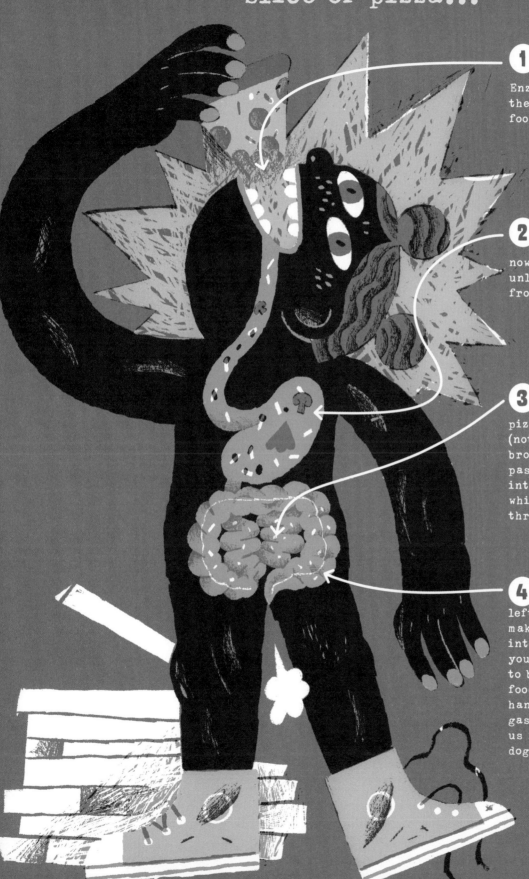

1 **FIRST YOU CHEW** the pizza into smaller bits. Enzymes in your saliva start their work of breaking the food apart.

2 **YOUR MUSCULAR STOMACH** churns your now-mushy pizza. More enzymes unlock groups of molecules from each other.

3 **NEXT STOP, SMALL INTESTINE,** where your pizza meets yet more enzymes (noticing a theme here?). The broken-down molecules of food pass through the walls of your intestine into your bloodstream, which delivers nutrients throughout your body.

4 **THE LARGE INTESTINE** is the last stop for what's left of your lunch before it makes its stinky way back out into the world. Here's where your resident bacteria get down to business, breaking up the food particles the enzymes can't handle. These bacteria, and the gases they make, are what make us fart. (No need to blame the dog anymore!)

WHEN THE BIGGEST ANIMAL DIES

Whales aren't just big. They're colossal. Blue whales, the largest animal ever to live, can be as long as a jumbo jet and weigh as much as 20 school buses. Their hearts are the size of a small car with arteries wide enough for a kid to swim through. **But if whales are larger than life, what happens when one dies?**

Normally, dead whales sink to the seafloor. If the water is shallow, the whale's body will be broken apart by scavengers relatively quickly, but if it falls into deeper water, the process can be much slower, sometimes taking up to 30 years!

1 Sharks and other meat eaters begin by stripping the flesh from the skeleton.

2 Next come the crabs, shrimp, and worms, some of which are specialists in breaking down whale bones (see page 56).

3 Finally, bacteria take over to finish the job.

BEACHED WHALE OR TICKING TIME BOMB?

When a whale dies, bacteria living in its body begin breaking down its organs and producing gases that cause the whale's body to bloat. These bloated giants can wash up on shore, swelling to twice their original size. **When this happens, decomposition can take an explosive turn.**

With nowhere for those gases to escape, pressure inside the whale builds and builds until—you guessed it—the putrefying carcass explodes like a fleshy Fourth of July firework. Take cover!

The Case of the Exploding Whale

A whale made its messy mark in Taiwan in 2004. When the whale died on a local beach, scientists loaded it on a truck to take it to a nearby university for study.

But the decomposition process was already well underway, and the bumps and jiggles of the road were too much for the behemoth to bear. As the truck traveled along a crowded city street, the whale's body exploded, covering shops, people, and cars with a shower of blood, blubber, and guts.

In another case, to help speed up the breakdown of a beached sperm whale in Oregon in 1970, officials decided to pack the lifeless giant with dynamite and blow it up into small chunks, thinking hungry seagulls and other animals would help clean up. Instead, people ended up running for their lives as **boulder-sized chunks of rotting blubber rained from the sky.**

Lesson learned: It's best to leave decomposition to the experts.

ROTTEN NESTS

You might know people who collect their food scraps or yard waste in a backyard compost pile. **But did you know that some animals compost, too?**

To make their nests, male Australian brush turkeys collect leaves and decaying matter from the forest floor to build compost mounds the size of a car. As these nesting materials begin to break down, the mound heats up from all the work being done by the busy decomposers within. Daddy Turkey checks the temperature of his hot rot pile by sticking his beak into it, and adds or takes away organic matter to keep things at a perfectly toasty 91 to 95°F (33 to 35°C).

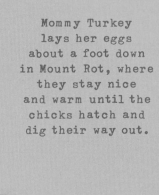

Mommy Turkey lays her eggs about a foot down in Mount Rot, where they stay nice and warm until the chicks hatch and dig their way out.

Alligator Bake

Alligators are also known to keep their eggs toasty and warm inside a rotting nest of compost. In fact, it's the temperature of the nest that will determine whether mama's scaly bundles of joy are male or female. A cooler nest (between 82 and 86°F/28 and 30°C) will produce female hatchlings, and a hot nest (between 90 and 93°F/32 and 34°C) will produce all males. A nest that falls in between will have some of each!

AS THE ROTTEN WORLD BURNS

Have you ever stopped to think about the oil-based gasoline we pump into cars, the gas that burns under a bubbling pot of pasta on a stove top, or the little black chunks of coal burned in the power plants that light many homes?

For better or worse, these things—known as fossil fuels—have shaped the modern world as we know it. **But where do fossil fuels come from, and what are they made of?**

I DID NOT SIGN UP FOR THIS

LET'S CUT TO THE CHASE: Oil, gas, and coal are made from the bodies of partially decayed plants and animals that died tens or even hundreds of millions of years ago.

1. Dead creatures were sealed away, along with the carbon-based energy still held in their bodies.

Locked-Up Energy

Just like plants today, ancient plants (and the animals that ate them) got their energy from the sun. When they died, that energy was locked in their bodies. Most of them were gobbled up and recycled back into the soil by ancient decomposers.

But the plants and tiny organisms that died in boggy or watery environments sank down and built up in layers over time, covered by sand, mud, and clay. These layers never fully decomposed because they were too acidic, and there wasn't enough oxygen.

2. Pressure, heat, and time transformed these remains into oil, natural gas, and coal.

3. For thousands of years, humans have been digging, drilling, and mining these fuels—and burning them to unlock their energy.

BURNING FOSSIL FUELS gives off carbon dioxide, methane, and other invisible gases that have been causing big changes in the earth's climate. That's why some people are now focusing on alternative sources of energy, like solar and wind power. **The sun and wind never run out**, and they cause less harm to the earth, its people, and its ecosystems.

THE ROT RESISTANCE

If decomposition is the breakdown of stuff that was either alive at some point or came from something living, what about everything else? Well, with some incredible exceptions, if something's not organic, decomposers can't eat it.

Let's take plastic. Plastics were only invented about 100 years ago, but they can take hundreds or even **thousands of years to break down**. Even then, certain plastics only break down into micro- (super small) or nano- (extra super small!) plastics.

These itty bitty bits might be too small to see with the naked eye, but they can add up to a big, bad impact on the health of animals and ecosystems.

Party Pooper

Think about it: Every single shiny mylar balloon at every party you've ever been to is still somewhere on the earth (probably in a landfill), looking deflated but otherwise very much like it did on party day.

When your great-great-great-great-great-great-great-great-great-great-great-great-great-great-great-grandchild (**yes, that's 15 greats**) is celebrating their own birthday, the balloons from your parties will finally be broken down into pieces small enough that they can no longer be seen with the naked eye.

How Long Does It Last?

Just how long do things stick around when decomposers aren't part of the breakdown plan? It depends whether they're buried in a landfill, floating around in the ocean, or hanging out on a forest floor. And for many things (especially plastics), it's still a bit of an educated guess.

Tin can (50—100 years)

Aluminum can (80—250 years)

Mylar party balloon (450 years)

Disposable diaper (500 years)

Plastic toothbrush (500 years)

Plastic toy (500—1,000 years)

Plastic bag (up to 10,000 years)

Glass bottle (1 million years)

Styrofoam (forever)

PLASTIC-EATING HUNGRY FUNGI

Wait! Scientists are discovering that some amazing decomposers might be able to help us with our plastic problem after all. The common and edible oyster mushroom, for example, makes enzymes that break down and digest certain kinds of plastic. In other words, certain hungry fungi can actually use plastics as food, converting them into the energy they need to grow. This is exciting, but plastic is still a major source of pollution.

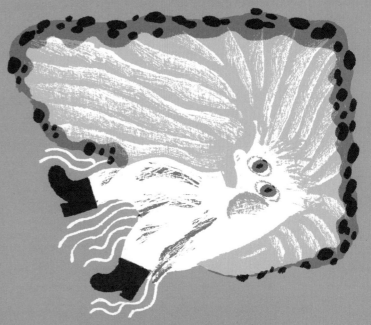

These **fungal wizards** are literally transforming polluting plastics into tasty mushroom meat!

Fungi and Bugs for the Win!

Scientists are also working on making new "super enzymes" that can break down plastics super fast, including one made from two enzymes found in plastic-eating bugs.

Part 3

MEET THE DECOMPOSERS

Decomposers are artists and magicians of decay, the essential crew behind the dirty work that keeps the world going. Some are slimy, others have shells. Some burrow and some buzz, while others crawl and creep. They're big; they're small; they're here, there, and everywhere. But what—or perhaps who—are they? It's time to meet the decomposers.

The decomposers on the following pages fall into three categories.

Saprotrophs include fungi and bacteria that use chemicals to break down the dead stuff. (Remember all those enzymes?) Some people consider them the only true decomposers.

Detritivores have good old internal digestive systems. While enzymes do play a role in digestion, there's a lot of physical breakdown that happens here through grinding, chewing, gnashing, and squeezing.

A support team helps make the conditions for decay just right by managing moisture and oxygen levels and moving decomposers around through the environment.

They are also one of the following:

Macro means visible to the naked eye

Micro means visible only with a microscope

ANTS

Detritivore / Support Team

Most of us think of ants as a picnic pest, arriving in a leggy line for their share of sweet watermelon and tasty sandwiches. Ants tend to be flexible eaters, munching on whatever they come across, including the dead stuff. In fact, ants play a super-important role in keeping the environment clean by feeding on dead insects, animals, and other organic waste. An army of ants can reduce a small carcass to bones in a matter of hours!

Ants that nest underground also play a role in decomposition by bringing other rot workers, like fungi and bacteria, down into the soil with them as they dig their elaborate **tunnels.**

Ants introduce **oxygen** (a key ingredient for rot) and mix up nutrients in the soil as much as earthworms do.

BACTERIA

Saprotroph

Bacteria are so tiny it would take more than 25,000 of them all lined up in a row to measure the length of a kid's thumb. A single pinch of healthy soil can be home to more than a billion bacteria of 10,000 different varieties. Not all bacteria are decomposers, and some can make people and animals very sick, but the rot-loving kind are certainly mighty when it comes to decomposition.

Bacteria are shaped like spirally twists, spheres, and rods, and they can get nutrients from pretty much everything imaginable. Wherever bacteria find themselves living, whether on the decaying remains of an animal, on a slab of Arctic ice, inside your body, or at the bottom of the ocean, chances are they'll be able to make an enzyme to digest what needs digesting.

YUCK!

1½"

25,000 bacteria could line up here!

Some bacteria can break down dangerous pollutants like chemical pesticides, herbicides, and heavy metals. Oil-eating bacteria are even used to help clean up oil spills.

41

BEETLES

Not all of the roughly 1.5 million different kinds of beetles on earth are decomposers. Ladybugs, for example, are beetles of the charming and dainty variety, feeding mostly on cute little aphids and sweet fruits. But what about the ladybug's poop-eating, flesh-hungry cousins? Beetles play many different roles in decomposition both as babies called grubs and as adults. If something is rotting, chances are there are beetles close by who want in on the action.

Carrion Beetles

Carrion is another word for the decaying flesh of a dead animal, so you can probably guess what these guys like to eat. Some carrion beetles like to nosh a bit, and then burrow inside their meal to lay their eggs. Others will use their tiny legs to dig out the soil around a dead animal so that it gets buried, hiding it from other hungry decomposers. These beetles also like to eat other decomposers, especially tasty, writhing maggot masses (see page 52). Mmmm.

Dung Beetles

Dung beetles are remarkable little poo gobblers. Most varieties have strong wings and can fly long distances in search of the perfect pile of poop.

Grown-up dung beetles suck out the stinky, nutritious liquid from their doo-doo dinner. They can also roll balls of dung up to 50 times their body weight. (That's like a 10-year-old human moving around a small car!) They take the dung back to their underground homes to use as food or as a nice cozy nest for their eggs. Baby dung beetles can chew, so they can munch on turds directly rather than just slurping up the poop soup like their parents do.

SLURP!

I'M DEAD

Skin Beetles

Skin beetles begin showing up on rotting animal bodies after they've had a chance to dry out. These scaled scurriers are great for breaking down not only dead flesh, but also the fur, hair, and feathers still hanging around later in the rot process. Museums and other bone collectors sometimes bring in skin beetles to clean off skeletons before displaying them.

Dead-Wood-Eating Beetles

Not all decomposer beetles go for the stinky stuff. Some prefer wood, which is good news because wood makes up a big chunk of all the dead organic matter on the planet at any given time. Beetles like long-horned beetles, powder-post beetles, and certain weevils play a big role in this work, munching up dead wood as both grubs and adults. Wood doesn't have many nutrients, so these beetles also eat the fungi living inside their woody meals.

BUTTERFLIES AND MOTHS

Detritivore /

When we think of butterflies, most of us picture graceful creatures fluttering from bloom to bloom in search of sweet nectar. But, as grown-ups so often like to remind you, you can't live entirely on sugar and—guess what?—neither can butterflies.

Seeking minerals and salts to balance out their diets, some will feed on tree sap, sweat, tears, urine, or even blood. Many butterflies also like to dine on death and decay.

Blue Morphos

Known as one of the most beautiful insects in the world, blue morphos don't drink nectar at all! Instead, they consume fermented (a.k.a. rotted) tree sap, liquified rotting fruit, and the fluids found in decaying animal carcasses.

Join the Puddle Club!

When lots of butterflies get together for a repugnant rot party—say on a giant poo pile, on top of a dead fish, or at a big stinky puddle—it's called a puddle club. True story. Think of it as a kind of super-gross community cookout. Don't forget your straw!

DUNG is another tasty treat for many butterflies, including red admirals, harvesters, viceroys, mourning cloaks, and question marks. To eat poop—or rather, to drink it—they stick their long mouthparts, called proboscises, into the turds and slurp up the juicy bits.

Moths have feathery antennae and are usually fuzzier and duller in color than their butterfly cousins. But what they have in common is a similar habit of snacking on gross stuff and playing a surprising role in the world of rot.

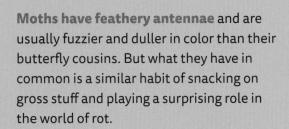

Tineid Moths

This is a family with broad tastes, ranging from animal bits like fur and feathers to poop, fungi, wool, and other natural fibers in your closet. Many in this group like to eat keratin, the difficult-to-break-down stuff of nails, hooves, and hair. **Gopher tortoise moths**, for example, live entirely on the keratin found in the shells of dead gopher tortoises.

Sloth Moths

For sloth moths, it all starts when a sloth climbs down from its tree for its weekly trip to the ground, which for the sloth is one giant bathroom. Mama moths living in its fur hop off to lay their eggs in the steamy poo pile. When the eggs hatch, the very hungry caterpillars nosh on the poop. After they build a cocoon and transform into adults, the moths flap their way up into the trees to find a nice furry sloth to live on.

CRUSTACEANS

 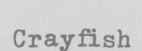

Crustaceans (*kruh-STAY-shinz*) are a complicated bunch of hard-shelled creatures. Some of them have sharp and powerful pinching claws, and others have none at all. A few, like krill, are tiny, while others, like spider crabs, are absolute giants. Although many crustaceans stick strictly to live food, others do have a taste for rot.

Crabs

Crabs will eat pretty much whatever they can find, including dead plants, animals, and waste. **Fiddler crabs** cruise the beaches when the tide is out, sifting through the sand and mud for bits of decay. **Japanese spider crabs** walk slowly along the ocean floor on their massive legs, which can span up to 12 feet across! They're searching for rotting fish, dead crustaceans, and other decaying sea goodies.

Crayfish

If you've ever splashed around in a stream or lake or mucked about in a swamp, you may have seen a crayfish. Some call these little creatures crawfish or crawdads, while others call them rock lobsters or mudbugs. No matter their name, they tend to hang out under rocks and love scarfing down dead leaves and other decomposing matter.

Giant Isopods

Giant isopods are super-sized, sea-dwelling versions of the pill bugs that live under the rocks in your neighborhood park (see page 61). The largest of them can be as big as a laptop. These adorable sea beasts feed on debris as it falls to the ocean floor.

Shrimp

Like crabs, shrimp will happily feed on most things they can fit into their mouths, including bits of plants and animals, algae, and bacteria. Living or dead, you ask? Either will do. Shrimp don't care! They also create a nice environment for other decomposers with their tasty, nutrient-rich poop. **Cleaner shrimp** set up cleaning stations in coral reefs where fish can show up to have bacteria and dead skin munched up off their bodies. Thanks, neighbors!

Lobsters

Most lobsters eat live food (watch out for those pinchy claws!), but some do dabble in death. The **squat lobster**, small enough to fit in the palm of your hand, feeds on particles of dead stuff collecting on the seafloor. When they find larger carcasses, they use their claws to tear them to bits and gulp down the flesh and organs.

EARTHWORMS

Detritivore / Support Team / ◉

From nightcrawlers to red wigglers, there are over three hundred different kinds of earthworms in North America alone. Some are puny, at just half the width of a pencil tip, while others are the length of 10 sticks of string cheese linked together! These slimy, slithering, eyeless, headless, toothless creatures can't hear or see, but they can perceive light and vibration.

Some people put worms to work in their homes. **Vermicomposting** (composting with worms) involves housing a colony of worms in a bin and feeding them food scraps that would otherwise end up in a landfill.

The channels and openings worms create in the ground allow oxygen and water to make their way into the soil more easily.

Different kinds of earthworms live in different parts of the soil. Some hang out at the surface while others dwell in **fancy burrows** up to 6 feet belowground, tunneling up to daylight when they're hungry.

Invasion of the Earthworms?

While earthworms are important decomposers, in North America many of them are what scientists call **non-native species**. Earthworms have been moved to places they've never lived before in their 200 million years on earth. They hitch rides as fishing bait, inside potted plants, and on shoes.

Some of these worms, like **crazy worms** (watch them squirm!), are so good at eating up leaf litter that they don't leave anything behind for all the other decomposers in the soil. Without a certain amount of debris on the forest floor, many insects and plants can't survive, and the interconnected systems they're part of get thrown out of whack.

WHO LET THE WORMS OUT?

BAIT

As worms gulp down soil, pebbles, and sand, they take in leaf fragments and other organic matter. They also swallow bacteria and other tiny decomposers in the soil. Along with special enzymes, it's these sidekicks that really get the rot party going.

Worm poop, or **castings**, are packed full of nutrients and minerals for plants to suck up. Each day an earthworm can digest an amount of food equal to its body weight. Can you imagine pooping out 80 to 100 pounds a day?

49

ECHINODERMS

Detritivore

feather star

What would you look like as an echinoderm? (Spoiler alert: The answer is *weird*. Definitely weird.)

The word **echinoderm** (eh-KINE-uh-derm) means "spiky skin." This family includes sea stars, sea urchins, sea cucumbers, and some lesser-known but still marvelous creatures like sea lilies, basket stars, feather stars, and brittle stars.

Many echinoderms are hunters (usually very slooooow hunters), but most also like to gobble up dead and decaying matter found clinging to rocks, floating around, and hanging out on the ocean floor.

Sea Stars

Sea stars (often called starfish) can be found across all of the world's oceans. Most are flexible eaters, preying on shellfish, sponges, and snails and munching on algae when it suits their fancy. Many are also detritivores because what's easier to catch than, well, dead stuff?

When sea stars get a whiff of something rotten, they move toward it at top speed (usually a few inches per minute). Eventually, that tasty dead thing may become the site of a wild sea-star feeding frenzy.

How Do Sea Stars Eat?

It's wonderfully weird. First, their mouths are on their undersides. (Imagine if your mouth were on the bottom of your foot!) Stranger still, they push their sacklike stomachs out through their mouths to rest on top of their food. Then they ooze special enzymes to break down the food while it's still outside their body. Once the food has been liquefied and absorbed, sea stars pull their loaded tummies back into their bodies and go about their business.

Next time you're swimming in the ocean, thank a sea star for barfing up its stomach to help keep the water clean for you.

OiNK?

sea pig

Sand Dollars

Sand dollars (those fun little
cookie-shaped discs you collect
at the beach) are actually a kind
of flat **sea urchin**. Like sea stars,
sand dollars and other urchins will eat a
variety of things, including little bits of dead
plants and animals suspended in water.

When a sand dollar reaches the end of
its life, it loses the velvety spines covering
its body and washes up on shore, where it's
bleached white by the sun.

Sea Cucumbers

Next time you see a cucumber at the grocery store,
imagine it as a squishy jelly blob covered in soft
spikes. Also, imagine that it's alive! Some species of
sea cucumber are no bigger than a human thumb,
while others can grow to be up to 6½ feet long!
Then there's the **sea pig**, whose name says it all.

When sea cucumbers eat, they extend beautiful
feathery tentacles or tube feet from their mouths.
Whatever gets caught in their frills—from algae to
tiny marine animals and waste—is brought into the
mouth. Sea cucumbers also tend to swallow sand
and sediment, filtering out the organic bits and
pooping out the rest. Nice work, detritivores!

sand dollar

purple sea urchin

51

FLIES

Detritivore

Can you imagine an army of ravenously hungry, flesh-eating babies, capable of breaking down most of a large mammal's body in under a week? This isn't a scary bedtime story; it's the real-life story of **maggots**, a.k.a. writhing, wormlike fly larvae.

Often the most obvious noise coming from a pile of rot is the buzz-buzz of flies. That's because a variety of flies and fly larvae have quite an appetite for rot, whether it be flesh, poop, or trash. Flies have an incredible sense of smell. Some kinds can catch the scent of an animal just seconds after its death and from more than 9 miles away.

Females lay eggs or larvae (depending on the kind of fly) directly on or in the rotting material. What a perfect nursery!

Most adult flies can only eat liquid foods, so they feed on the fluids of decaying animal bodies, poop, and other rotting matter.

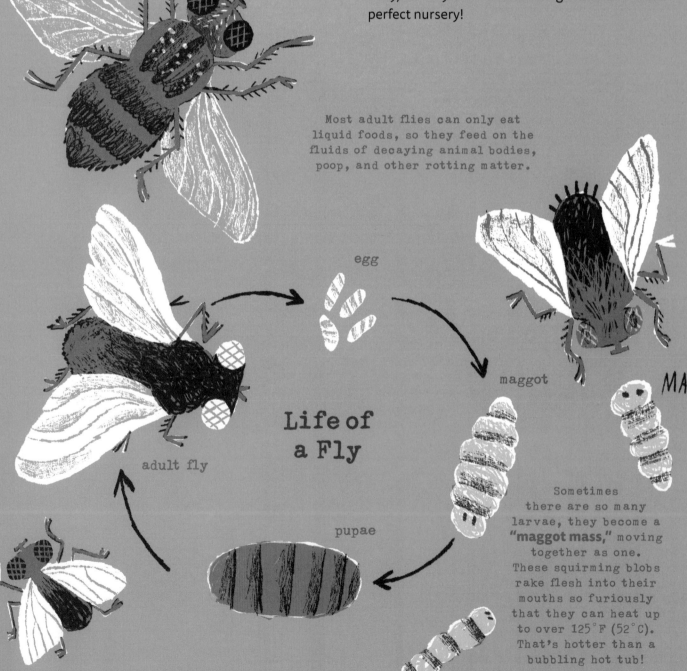

egg

maggot

MA?

Life of a Fly

adult fly

pupae

Sometimes there are so many larvae, they become a **"maggot mass,"** moving together as one. These squirming blobs rake flesh into their mouths so furiously that they can heat up to over 125°F (52°C). That's hotter than a bubbling hot tub!

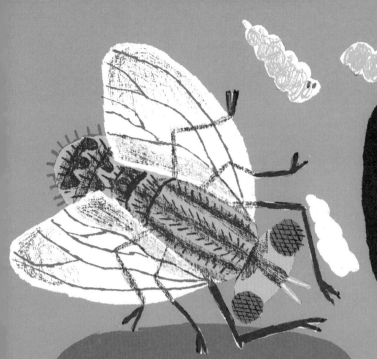

Blowflies

These common, medium-size, metallic-colored flies prefer to eat dead animals and garbage. Some blowfly larvae are used in **maggot therapy,** in which a doctor sprinkles freshly emerged (and sanitized) maggots onto certain kinds of wounds that aren't healing on their own. The maggots gobble up all of the dead and decomposing flesh, leaving behind a clean wound with a better chance of healing. Gross, but true!

Flesh Flies

These buzzers lay squirmy larvae instead of eggs and prefer to feed on and in dung, decaying animal bodies, and open wounds (hence their name). Eww.

Vinegar Flies

Also known as fruit flies, these tiny insects are found in and around rotting fruits.

Black Soldier Flies

These flies are experts at helping out with household composting. Also, unlike many other kinds of flies, these guys don't carry diseases and filth. They actually help keep decomposing matter smelling fresher!

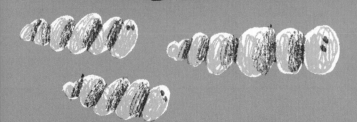

FUNGI

Saprotroph /

Mushrooms are just a tiny part—the fruit, in fact—of larger organisms called fungi. The rest of the fungus usually lives where we can't see it, like belowground or deep inside a log. Though silent and stealthy, fungi are some of the most important decomposers around, especially in forests.

Fungi can't make their own food like plants do, but have you ever seen a mushroom walking around looking for food? Fungi eat things that don't move. And what's good at not moving? Dead stuff!

Not all fungi are death-eating decomposers, but the ones that are break down a wide range of things, from dead plants and enormous tree trunks to hair, bones, hooves, and even rocks. "But wait, fungi don't have mouths," you might be saying. So how do they do it? Fungi ooze enzymes that break down the dead stuff into simpler forms. Then, branching, threadlike structures called **hyphae** suck up the nutrients.

Hyphae—known as **mycelium** when in large groups— are also what let fungi push themselves deep into rotting stuff, like an enormous fallen tree trunk.

Decomposer Piggybackers

What do you call a fungus that breaks down another decomposer fungus? A piggybacker, of course! One example is the **ochre cushion fungus**, which grows out of birch polypore mushrooms, and decomposes them after they've done their part to break down a piece of dead birch wood.

Chicken of the Woods

No, these chickens don't cluck like their feathered namesakes, but they do cause foragers to cry out in delight. These edible fungal fruits grow out of decaying tree trunks like wavy, chicken-flavored fans in bright orange and yellow. (Remember, never eat a foraged mushroom unless an expert tells you it's safe!)

Stinkhorns

Stinkhorns are usually smelled before they are seen. Giving off the fine aroma of putrefying flesh and dung, these bizarre-looking mushrooms pop up from wood chips and other dead wood, rotting leaves, and soil.

MARINE WORMS

Not all worms live in the soil. In fact, marine worms are among the most common animals in the salty seas. **Polychaetes** (PAH-lee-keets) are a family of about 10,000 different kinds of marine worms whose bodies are covered in tiny hairlike bristles.

Zombie Worms

Zombie worms, no longer than a pointer finger, have no mouth or stomach, yet they specialize in breaking down enormous bones, including those of whales. When other decomposers have eaten up the softer bits of a **whale fall**, zombie worms come in to clean up the skeletal remains.

Zombie worms first drill into the bone with special plantlike "roots." Then they leak out a **bone-dissolving acid** to free the tasty stuff inside so that bacteria living on the worms' roots can digest it. Scientists don't yet fully understand how those nutrients transfer from the bacteria to the zombie worms, but they're working on it.

Christmas Tree Worms

Twinkling among coral reefs in shades of red, orange, pink, blue, and white, Christmas tree worms tunnel down inside special tubes they've made for themselves. When they need oxygen or dinner, they peek out of their tubes and use their tentacles to move food toward their mouth.

Sea Mice

A sea mouse is a fuzzy, gray, oval-shaped marine worm that looks a lot like, well, a wet mouse (though some are much more brightly colored). These aquatic cuties get their looks thanks to a thick covering of long, bristly hairs, which get coated with mud and silt as they creep along shallow seafloors searching for food. What's on the menu? Rotting animals, among other things.

MILLIPEDES

Detritivore

You may not always love eating veggies, but millipedes sure do—as long as they're rotten. Millipedes have played a role in the decomposition of plant matter since before dinosaurs roamed the earth. They live in the soil, where they use their strong jaws to chew up leaf litter, dead wood, and other decaying plant parts. They ooze saliva from their jaws to soften their food, then scrape it into their mouths.

What about Centipedes?

Centipedes sometimes hang out with decomposers, but unlike millipedes, they only eat animals—live ones!

Millipedes have between 40 and 800 legs.

Inside the millipede's digestive system are more decomposers, like fungi, bacteria, and nematodes, ready to help break things down before they're returned to the soil in a more usable form.

MITES

Detritivore / 👁 / 🔬

What creeps and crawls, has eight legs, and isn't a spider? A mite! People don't talk much about these critters, but they play a super-important role in breaking down dead animal cells.

Part of the reason mites aren't at the top of everyone's mind (even though they are literally all over our bodies) is that they are small. While most mites are around the size of a pencil tip, many are microscopic. Out of sight, out of mind!

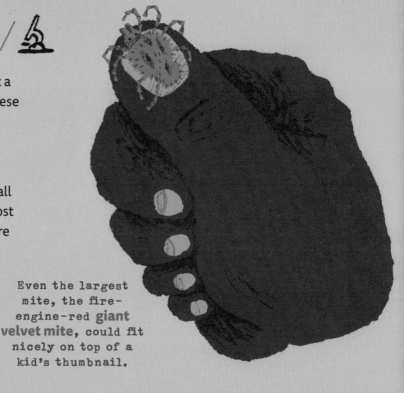

Even the largest mite, the fire-engine-red **giant velvet mite,** could fit nicely on top of a kid's thumbnail.

Make Yourself at Home!

Mites make their homes in some interesting places. Some species live on human eyelashes and eyebrows. (Don't worry, they're harmless!) And billions take up residence in our houses, where they gobble up flakes of dead skin (see page 23).

Other mites prefer to set up shop in bird nests and compost bins, while still others hang out in the soil. And many species of mites use rotting carcasses as their temporary habitats. No need to order takeout!

HOP ON!

Going My Way?

If mites are so tiny, how do they get themselves to the carcass buffet? Many mites are **hitchhikers,** clinging to the bodies of animals and insects (flies make great pilots). When their ride arrives at the rot party, the mites detach themselves and get to work.

MOLLUSKS

Detritivore

Soft-bodied mollusks, some of which have fancy shells for protection, can live either on land (see page 64) or in water environments. They come in many varieties and can be found burrowing, crawling, slithering, and swimming all around the world.

So which ones are decomposers and why?

Sea Snails and Slugs

Inside the beautiful, spiraling **conch** shell lives a snail that sometimes eats detritus found in sand. Some sea snails have a taste for the remains of dead animals, too.

Sea slugs don't have the fancy shells, and most eat live food, but the super-cool **ragged sea hare** can be found grazing on detritus-covered sand and mud in calm waters.

Bivalves

Bivalves like clams, mussels, and oysters have hard shells that open and close like a door on a hinge. They take in water for both breathing and eating through little slits in their flesh called gills. Certain bivalves are so good at breaking down the yucky stuff that they're used to clean up harmful pollutants in bays and harbors.

conch

ragged sea hare

Vampire Squids

All squids (and octopuses, too!) are mollusks, but only a few help out with decomposition. One is the **vampire squid**, which drifts about in the dark depths of the ocean gulping down marine "snow" made from flakes of dead animals, plants, and poop.

NEMATODES

Detritivore / Support Team

Nematodes or roundworms are long and slender. They've been known to squirm and wiggle, but they aren't related to earthworms. Most of them are microscopic, although, like earthworms, some can get alarmingly large (up to 23 feet long)!

Oh, and there are a lot of them. For every human on earth, there are about 60 billion nematodes. That means **8 out of 10** living animals on the planet are nematodes. They live pretty much everywhere: in fresh water and salt water, inside plants and animals, in the soil, and even down in the deepest cracks in the crust of the planet.

The kind of nematodes that lend a hand (or, rather, a strawlike mouthpart called a **stylet**) in decomposition are referred to as **free living**. This means that they don't live inside plants or animals, but on their own in soil, sand, and mud.

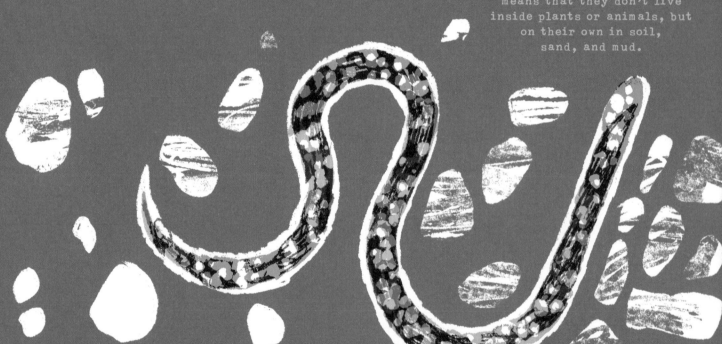

Support-Team Pride

Nematodes are star players on the decomposer support team. They feed on living fungi and bacteria, helping these decomposers spread by giving them a free ride in their digestive systems. Nematodes also tend to eat more than they need and then ooze out the leftovers in the form of simple, usable nutrients that plants can drink up through their roots.

PILL BUGS AND SOW BUGS

You may know them better as roly-polies or maybe potato bugs, but pill bugs—and their pals sow bugs—aren't bugs at all. These funny little isopods are landlubber crustaceans, which puts them in the same family as shrimp.

While both pill bugs and sow bugs are a type of **wood louse**, only one (can you guess which?) rolls up into a cute little ball when it's bothered.

Both pill bugs and sow bugs can be found hanging out in dark, damp places like under rotting logs, fallen leaves, and rocks, where they feed on decaying plants, fungi, and other rotten stuff.

Sometimes isopods hang out in their mama's underbelly pouch (called a **marsupium**) after hatching, kind of like kangaroo babies. Oh, and they eat their own poop and can drink from both their front and back ends.

PROTOZOA

Saprotroph

Protozoa (pro-toh-ZOH-uh) are ancient little creatures, some of which have been around for billions of years. Each one is made up of just a **single cell**. (For comparison, a human is made up of about 30 trillion cells!) Most protozoa are too tiny to see without a microscope, and they come in lots of strange shapes.

Some protozoa are a bit like accidental decomposers. Let's take one type—**paramecia** (pair-uh-MEE-see-uh)—as an example. These water-dwellers like to eat other decomposers, especially bacteria. They swim around using tiny hairlike threads to sweep food toward their mouth slits. They take in all the nutrients those yummy bacteria have been munching on and break them down further.

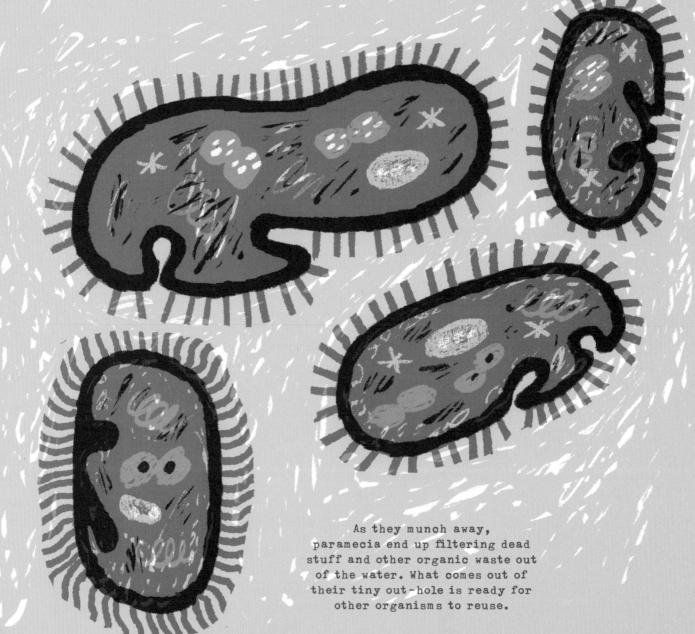

As they munch away, paramecia end up filtering dead stuff and other organic waste out of the water. What comes out of their tiny out-hole is ready for other organisms to reuse.

62

SLIME MOLDS

Saprotroph / 👁 / 🔬

There are about a thousand different kinds of slime molds, and—get this—not one of them is actual slime or actual mold. Scientists group them with simple organisms called protists, but these oddballs have a hard time fitting in anywhere.

While these slow creepers do feed directly on decaying matter, they also help out with the rot process by feeding on all the tasty bacteria and fungi that thrive on decay. The "fruiting bodies" of slime molds come in a rainbow of colors and in the wackiest shapes imaginable.

The blob slime mold (yes, that's really what it's called), is made up of millions of single cells all grouped together into one giant **supercell**. The biggest supercells can cover the floor of a single-car garage.

the blob

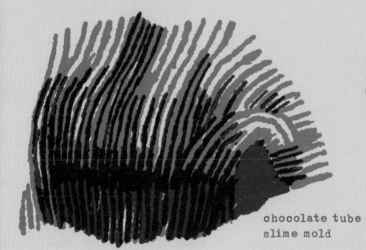
chocolate tube slime mold

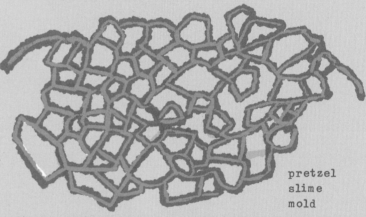
pretzel slime mold

carnival candy slime mold

Aliens at Home

How does a mouthless, brainless mass of cells eat? The cells at the front spread out like a fan, and when they find food, they engulf it, wrapping themselves around it to bring it into their bodies for digestion.

Slime molds may sound like something from outer space, but you can find them in some pretty basic places if you look closely. They grow on rotting logs (try cracking off a piece of bark and looking underneath), on mulch, in lawns, and on decaying leaves.

SLUGS AND SNAILS

Detritivore

Like many decomposers, slugs and snails are all around us, in cities and towns, forests, fields, wetlands, and even in deserts. You've probably seen them, soft and slimy, moving verrrry slowly across a sidewalk or trail in search of some delicious decay. Sometimes we see only what they've left behind: a trail of slime leading out of the garden.

Both snails and slugs live their lives close to the ground (or beneath it), and can be found either snuggling under rocks, logs, tree bark, and fallen leaves or exploring the upper soil zone of forest floors.

Some slugs and snails are hunters (others even cannibals!), but those that are decomposers have wide-ranging appetites. Some have even been known to consume empty shells, bones, antlers, and rock particles—including those of tombstones.

Slug Breakdown

Slugs have a tonguelike organ called a **radula** that's covered in thousands of tiny teeth. The radula breaks off bits of food and draws them in for digestion in a process called **rasping**. If you hold a slug or snail in your hand, you might feel it rasping on your skin. It feels like rubbing a tiny piece of sandpaper.

The actual breakdown begins in the mouth with saliva.

Deeper inside the body, bacteria and enzymes break things down even further into pieces that can be returned to the soil and sucked up by plant roots.

AAAAAA

Calcium Snacks

Snails play an extra-super-cool role in breaking down calcium and moving it through ecosystems. When snails eat dead leaves and wood, they break the calcium bits apart from the other stuff and store it in their shells.

When a turtle, salamander, mammal, or bird has a little snail snack, it comes with a serving of calcium. In this way, snails pass calcium up the food chain.

SPRINGTAILS

Detritivore / 👁

Springtails are roughly the length of a crayon tip. They get their name from the forked structure on their bellies that catapults them into the air when danger is near.

Springtails tend to hang out in large groups where there is plenty of food: in mulch, under rocks and decaying leaves and wood, and near moist soil—even in potted houseplants.

Not all springtails are decomposers, but those that are like to munch on decaying plant and fungal matter, including certain molds.

Snow Fleas

What's one (literally) cool place you might run into a springtail? Next time the winter snow begins to melt, peek outside near some tree trunks. You might see snow fleas jumping around on the surface of the snow looking for some rotten food to munch on. Snow fleas are not really fleas but a bluish-black type of springtail.

These jumpers really do look like they're partying!

TERMITES

Detritivore

You've probably heard of termites munching on wooden houses and furniture, slowly reducing them to dust. But what's so tasty about wood? These insects are after a substance called **cellulose**, which they find not only in decaying wood but also in dead grass, leaves, paper, and cardboard.

Termites are especially important as decomposers in deserts, where they can make huge mounds. With the help of special enzymes in their guts and some pretty wild protozoa or bacteria (depending on the type of termite), they're able to keep nutrient recycling going even when it's super dry.

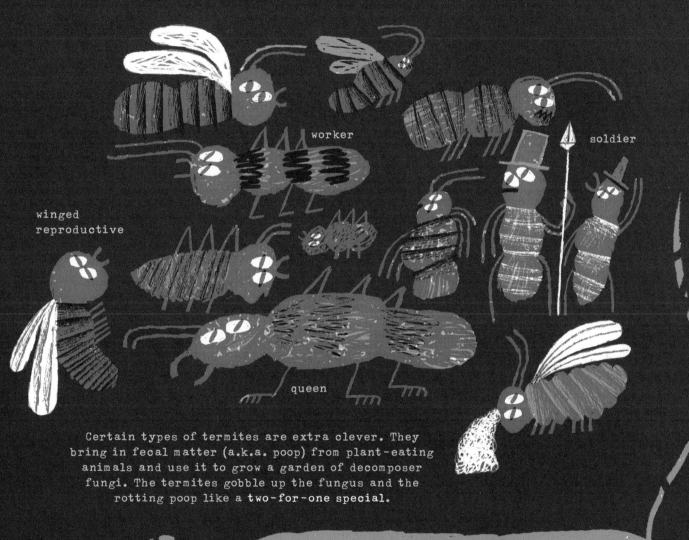

worker

soldier

winged reproductive

queen

Certain types of termites are extra clever. They bring in fecal matter (a.k.a. poop) from plant-eating animals and use it to grow a garden of decomposer fungi. The termites gobble up the fungus and the rotting poop like a **two-for-one special**.

Strangest Dinner Party Ever

Termites, like bees and ants, are social insects. This means that they live together in big families and have different jobs. The workers go out and munch on all the dead stuff. Then they transfer the nutrients to others who have been busy doing their own jobs.

They do this by creating a kind of pasty substance and spitting it into the mouths of their relatives or—get this—pushing it in droplet form out of their butts for others to lick up directly from the source.

ROTTEN ACTIVITIES, EXPLORATIONS & EXPERIMENTS

By now it should be clear that there is much in this rotten world of ours to be explored. And what better way to really dive into the rot than with some hands-on activities? With the help of your senses and a few basic materials you should be able to find around your house, you can put your ideas to the test, watch decomposition as it happens in real time, and even get to know a few decomposers.

Rotten Banana Experiment

Instead of saving those spotty bananas on the kitchen counter for banana bread, why not use them to conduct a rotten experiment? You'll need a ripe banana, two ziplock bags, and a spoonful of instant bread yeast (from the baking aisle at the grocery store).

1. Peel the banana and cut it in half.

2. Place each half into its own ziplock bag.

3. Sprinkle a big spoonful of instant bread yeast into one bag to cover the banana. Leave the other bag as is.

4. Seal your bags and let the breakdown begin!

5. Check in on your bananas over the next six to eight days. What do they look like? How are they changing? Do the processes happening inside the two bags look the same or different? Why? Does the yeast have any effect on the plastic bags? Why or why not?

Play Around with the Where of Rot

Test out how quickly or slowly things rot in different environments by creating your own handheld worlds of rot. Adjust the oxygen, moisture, and temperature of each miniature world to mimic the conditions of a desert, a rain forest, a bog, or something entirely different!

ZOMBIE SANDWICH STRIKES AGAIN

1. Gather three to five containers. Clean jars, old plastic takeout containers, or plastic food-storage containers will all work well.

2. Find something rottable (think leftovers from the fridge or a handful of leaves). Add a bit to each container.

3. Now play around with the oxygen, moisture, and temperature for each container. For example, keep one container hot and dry like a desert and another wet and warm like a rain forest. What happens if you flood one with water? How does the rot process change if you keep the lid on one container, take the lid off another, and poke holes in the lid of another?

4. Keep an eye on your containers over the next week or two, and chart your observations. Can you see decomposition happening in any of the containers? Which container gets an A+ for putrefaction? Where in your home or out in the wide world of rot might you find a place with conditions similar to those in your winning container?

Dig in the Dirt

Decomposing plant matter can be much more approachable than, say, a flattened skunk on your school bus route. Next time you pass a pile of fallen leaves, pick some up. Rub them between your fingers. Give them a whiff. What do you notice? Do the decomposing leaves have a smell?

Use your fingers or a stick to dig down under the leaves. What (or who) can you find there?

Jar o' Worms

Worms are one decomposer that you can easily observe in action, with just a few basic supplies and a little curiosity. You'll need a large jar (a clean pasta-sauce jar works well), a handful of small rocks, a scoop of soil, and a scoop of sand.

HELLO!

1. Add the small rocks to the jar until the bottom is covered.

2. Add a layer of soil, then a layer of sand, and continue with this pattern until only a few inches of space remain at the top. The top layer should be soil.

3. Get outside and dig for worms! They might be a little slimy, but they can't hurt you. Be brave and carefully place them into their new home.

4. Spray the soil with water, and add a small amount of vegetable scraps at the top of the jar. Fallen leaves will also work.

5. Cover the jar with a lid, a piece of foil, or a scrap of paper secured with a rubber band, making sure there are air holes for the worms. Place it in a dark spot.

6. Check in on your worm experiment in the coming days and weeks. What do you notice? Are there any tunnels? Have the worms been eating the food? Can you spot their castings?

Make a Fly Trap

Have you ever heard the old saying "You'll catch more flies with honey than with vinegar"? Well, by making a simple trap with a bit of honey in it, you may indeed catch a fly or two and get the chance to see these busy rot-revelers up close.

You'll need a serrated knife (to be used with the help of a grown-up), a plastic bottle (a single-serving water bottle will do the trick), about ¼ cup of honey, and some tape. To repeat the experiment, you'll need other bait like rotting meat or fruit.

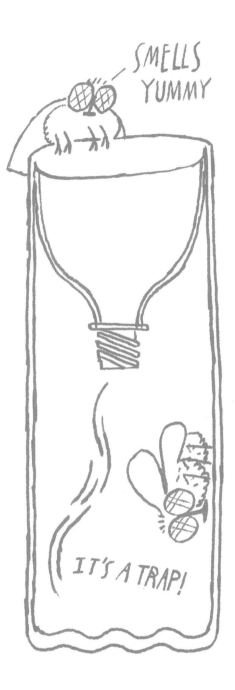

1. With a grown-up's help, use the serrated knife to cut off the top of the bottle, just below where it starts to narrow. Set the top aside.

2. Add the honey (or another sweet liquid) to the bottom of the bottle.

3. Turn the top part of the bottle upside down and place it into the bottom half of the bottle so the cut edges line up. Secure the edges together with tape.

4. Place the bottle somewhere you've seen flies before, either inside or outside. Check it regularly to see how many different kinds of flies you've caught.

5. Repeat the experiment with different kinds of bait, such as rotting meat or fruit. Do you attract more flies? Fewer flies? Different kinds of flies?

Note: Dead flies are also easy to find in window frames around your school or home. Check your windows for dead decomposers and break out a magnifying glass for a close-up inspection!

Roly-Poly Pets

When most people think of pets, they imagine puppies or kittens, but why not consider keeping a pill bug (a.k.a. roly-poly) or two as a pet? What better chance to observe decomposers at work? You'll need a large glass jar or terrarium.

1. Cover the bottom of your jar with moist soil. If you're feeling fancy, you can even plant a mini fern or some moss from your yard or a local garden store.

2. Head outside to collect some fallen leaves and bark. Add a layer of each on top of the soil. You can also add a few twigs and pebbles to help your roly-polies feel at home.

3. Now start flipping over rocks and logs on the ground to look for your new pets. Gently pick up a few cute little roly-polies with your fingers. (Don't worry! They can't bite, sting, or spread disease.) Place them in their new home.

4. Pick out names! You might consider Queen Rot, Uncle Fester, or perhaps Professor Decay?

5. Back inside, fill a spray bottle with water and gently mist your decomposers' habitat. You'll want to do this every day.

6. Feed your roly-polies fruit and vegetable scraps or leaf litter from outside regularly, and record your observations. Roly-polies are nocturnal, so they're likely to be busy munching on their rotten snacks while you're asleep.

FANCY HOUSE!

How to Catch a Garden Snail

If you want to get some face-to-face slime time, there are a few ways to go about it. You can buy slug bait and traps at gardening stores, but then you'll end up with a bunch of dead decomposers. These mucousy friends may be eating your plants, but they still have important work to do in their ecosystems, so traps that won't harm them are better for everyone.

After you've observed the slugs or snails up close (use a magnifying glass, if you have one), just let them go free again.

OPTION 1: If you have a garden or any potted plants outside, go out after dark when slugs and snails are most active and inspect the leaves with a flashlight. They especially love marigolds, basil, and strawberries.

OPTION 2: You can bait your local snails with some tasty cabbage, another favorite for these raspers. Leave the head of cabbage on the ground near some leafy plants, and come back the next day to see what kind of slimy sidekicks are hanging around.

OPTION 3: Place a wooden board on top of some soil in your yard or in a nearby park. Flip it over in the morning to see who's clinging on.

Index

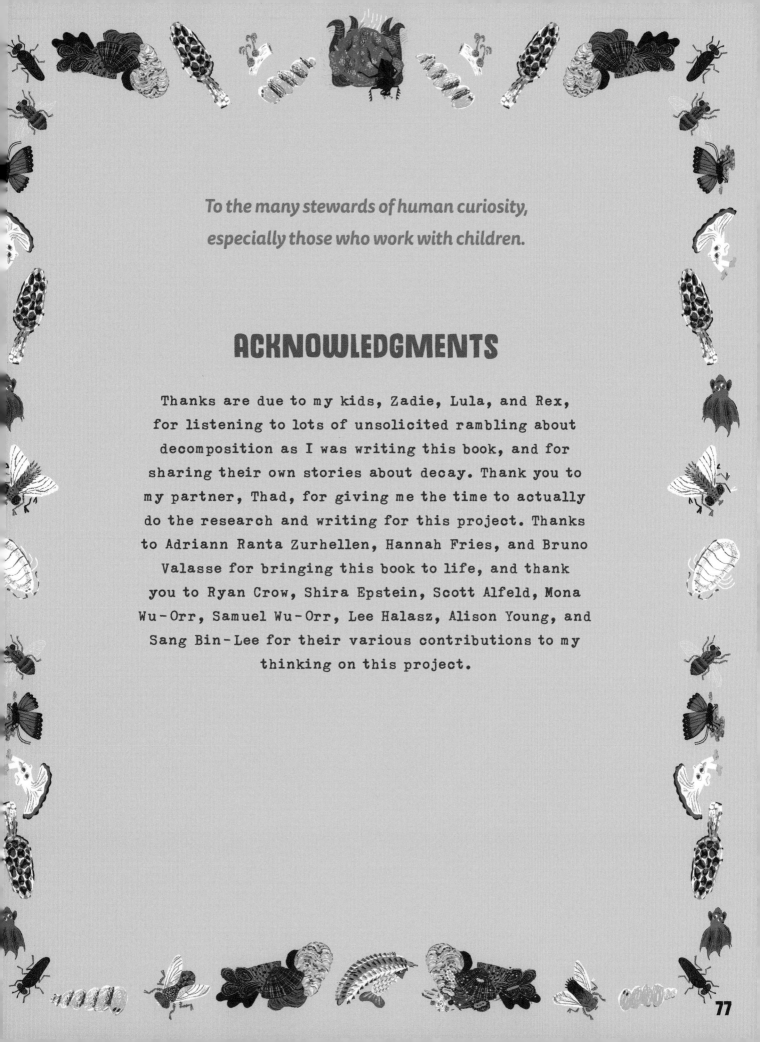

*To the many stewards of human curiosity,
especially those who work with children.*

ACKNOWLEDGMENTS

Thanks are due to my kids, Zadie, Lula, and Rex,
for listening to lots of unsolicited rambling about
decomposition as I was writing this book, and for
sharing their own stories about decay. Thank you to
my partner, Thad, for giving me the time to actually
do the research and writing for this project. Thanks
to Adriann Ranta Zurhellen, Hannah Fries, and Bruno
Valasse for bringing this book to life, and thank
you to Ryan Crow, Shira Epstein, Scott Alfeld, Mona
Wu-Orr, Samuel Wu-Orr, Lee Halasz, Alison Young, and
Sang Bin-Lee for their various contributions to my
thinking on this project.

The mission of Storey Publishing is to serve our customers by publishing practical information that encourages personal independence in harmony with the environment.

Edited by Hannah Fries

Book design by Michaela Jebb

Art direction by Michaela Jebb and Jessica Armstrong

Text production by Jennifer Jepson Smith

Illustrations by © Bruno Valasse

Storey Publishing

210 MASS MoCA Way

North Adams, MA 01247

storey.com

Storey Publishing is an imprint of Workman Publishing, a division of Hachette Book Group, Inc., 1290 Avenue of the Americas, New York, NY 10104. The Storey Publishing name and logo are registered trademarks of Hachette Book Group, Inc.

Distributed in Europe by Hachette Livre, 58 rue Jean Bleuzen, 92 178 Vanves Cedex, France

Distributed in the United Kingdom by Hachette Book Group, UK, Carmelite House, 50 Victoria Embankment, London EC4Y 0DZ

ISBNs: 978-1-63586-669-8 (paper over board); 978-1-63586-670-4 (fixed format EPUB); 978-1-63586-898-2 (fixed format PDF); 978-1-63586-897-5 (fixed format Kindle)

Printed in China by R. R. Donnelley on paper from responsible sources

10   9   8   7   6   5   4   3   2   1

RRD-S

Library of Congress Cataloging-in-Publication Data on file